Ever Changing Birmingham In Colour

By Garry Yates

Copyright IRWELL PRESS Ltd.,
ISBN 978-1-906919-66-5
First published in 2014 by Irwell Press Ltd., 59A, High
Street, Clophill, Bedfordshire, MK45 4BE
Printed by 1010, China

I was born in the Handsworth district of Birmingham in 1954 and today I still only live one mile away from where I was born. Growing up in the 1960s I witnessed innumerable changes to the Birmingham skyline, because perhaps more than any other city at the time, Birmingham replaced numerous terraced and back-to-back houses with multi-storey tower blocks reaching a total of 444 across the city, including the new district of Chelmsley Wood. All remaining gas street lighting was replaced by electric lighting, and in the city centre the Inner Ring Road was constructed which swept away many smaller roads and buildings, some of which like the former Josiah Mason College at Paradise Circus would, today, have been listed buildings. The Bull Ring Shopping Centre, (the first indoor shopping centre in the country) opened in 1964 and the Post Office Tower (as it was known then) in Lionel Street became the city's first tall landmark. However over the years many of these so called 'improvements' came to be seen as not very 'improving' at all, or were otherwise unsuccessful or deficient. Times and attitudes change and many tower blocks are now being demolished in favour of ground level housing schemes and apartments. In the city centre the Inner Ring Road with its numerous subways, known as the 'Concrete Collar' was restricting outward growth of the city centre, and is now slowly being removed as are the unpopular subways; the largest part of this scheme so far is the rebuilding of the Bull Ring and the surrounding area. In recent years many apartment blocks have been built in the city centre especially around the canal network and many more schemes have been planned or started, but at the moment some are on hold due to the effects of the recent recession – hopefully most will be completed, but some will not.

In order to help with locating the buildings and streets in the photographs, I have put the pictures in an order based on a journey starting at Five Ways Island at the western end of Broad Street, heading down Broad Street into the city centre, and then in a clockwise direction, as close as possible, around the centre, and finally heading back towards Five Ways. The latter section of the book covers landmarks outside the city centre like the Birmingham Mint and HP Sauce factory, and again I have placed them in the order of a clockwise travelling direction starting at Hockley with the Birmingham Mint. This section of the book sadly indicates how much industry has been lost in Birmingham over the last forty years including brewing and engineering and more recently bread making, with closure of the Hovis Works at Garretts Green and the subsequent loss of jobs. Hopefully many people reading this book will have fond memories of these buildings and landmarks, some relatively young, that have all disappeared within the last four decades.
G. M. Yates, 2013

The Edgbaston Shopping Centre, built in the 1960s, was a popular venue for many years, but became run down in the 1990s, and the 14 storey Calthorpe House office block had already been vacated by 2006 when this picture was taken. Seen from the Hagley Road, the centre was well known for a public house called 'The Unspoilt by Progress' the slogan used by Banks's Brewery who ran the pub. Like many other tower blocks, this one was brought down by a controlled demolition using explosives on Sunday 9th March 2008 and the site was scheduled to be redeveloped with shops, offices and apartments, although due to the troubled economy, the 'Edgbaston Galleries' scheme was scrapped. The area is now home to a Morrisons supermarket and some smaller shops.

Birmingham's Children's Hospital on Ladywood Middleway, in 1998. It replaced a smaller Hospital in Steelhouse Lane (dating back to 1862) and was opened by King George V and Queen Mary on 21st May 1919. The Ladywood Hospital site closed in1996 and moved back to a heavily refurbished General Hospital in Steelhouse Lane, returning to its former home after 130 years. The new Children's Hospital was opened by Lady Diana Spencer before her untimely death and the former hospital was demolished, retaining the front elevation. Behind the original facade is now an entertainment complex consisting of bars, restaurants and cinemas, with an underground car park. Tricorn House on Hagley Road can be seen in the background.

This 1994 view down Broad Street from Ryland Street looking across to Bishopgate Street shows the buildings which used to occupy the site which has now become the Five Ways entertainment complex, with shops, bars and the Cineworld complex opposite. In recent times the latter has played host to several film premiers. The multi-storey Cumberland House in the background is scheduled to be converted into a hotel with offices associated. The pavement to the left has in recent years become home to Birmingham's 'Walk of Stars' similar to the Hollywood style pavement stars. One-time rock star, bat enthusiast and now advice columnist Ozzy Osbourne of Aston was the first to be honoured, in July 2007, and since then stars such as comedian Jasper Carrott, Noddy Holder from the band 'Slade', Murray Walker the motor racing commentator and Chris Tarrant, game show host, have been added.

Broad Street in 1988, showing the former Bush House, on the corner of Cumberland Street, which were the main offices for Birmingham City Council housing department at the time. Dating from the 1950s, the building was well known among Birmingham residents, as anything to do with council bills/enquiries were dealt with here. The building was swept away in late 1989 to make way for the redevelopment of Broad Street and today is home to a Novotel and multi-storey office blocks, and the BRMB Radio (now 'Free Radio') studios.

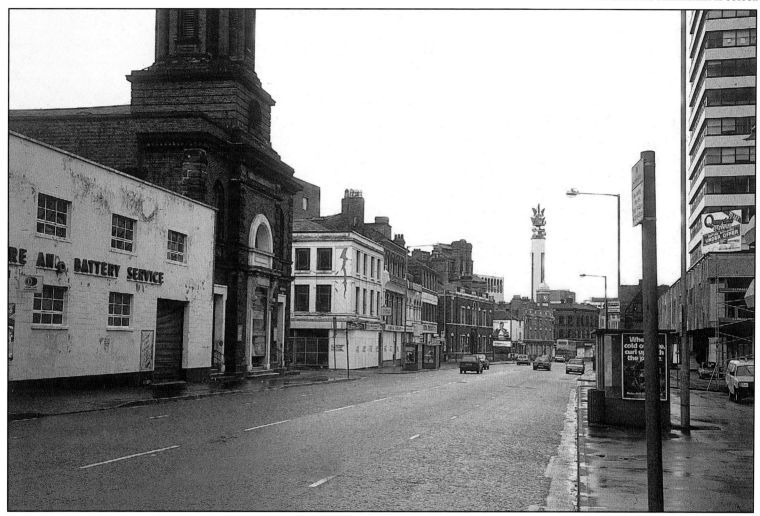

Broad Street looking towards the city centre shows how run-down the street had become before the redevelopment. Buildings which still remain on the left are the Crown public house, and the 2nd Church of Christ Scientist in Birmingham, now 'Flares' nightclub. Maybe the name is deliberately suggestive of hellfire, maybe it really refers to trousers... Many of the other buildings, some listed, have been refurbished while others have been swept away and replaced by offices, pubs, clubs and restaurants. These are now the hub of the city's nightlife especially on Friday and Saturday nights.

Oozells Street in 1982 and the former Atlas Works, home to bedding manufacturers T.E. Wales & Sons until 1958. In later years part of the building had been used as the Motor Vehicle Taxation Office. This area is now in the middle of the Oozells Square development with its Italian style piazza and fountains – a contrast indeed.

Stratford House in Broad Street in 1980, an antiques shop with a timber frame 'look' that was not as old as it seemed. Next to this used to be the Church of Messiah built over the canal – this was demolished in 1978. Sandwiched between St. Martins Row and St. Peters Place, this well known landmark was removed to make way for the enlarged entrance area to the Crown pub alongside the canal. The Brewmasters House in the background dating from 1805 was restored in 1984, and has been preserved as part of the Convention Centre development.

Looking from Broad Street down King Edwards Place in 1979, The Crown can be seen on the left, with Galton Tower in Cambridge Street, in the background. This road has now completely disappeared with the construction of the International Convention Centre (ICC) in 1989/1990, as did the antiques warehouse building and the Victorian cast-iron open-air toilet, once a common feature around the city. The main Symphony Hall now sits across this site with conference halls occupying the land in the distance.

This 1984 view of Broad Street looking towards the city centre shows the buildings in front of the old Bingley Hall. The road to the left is King Edwards Place with The Crown on the opposite corner, where Henry Mitchell began producing a noted homebrew in 1875 before the formation of the Mitchells and Butlers brewery in nearby Smethwick, another landmark recently demolished and replaced by a housing estate. Broadway 66 was a popular late night burger bar complete with early space invader machines! Note the Austin Maxi car, and the old style Broad Street lamp-posts, two of which can now be found at the Crich Tramway Museum, in front of the rebuilt Derby Assembly Rooms. This view today comprises the side entrance of the International Convention Centre with a bridge across the road linking the Hyatt Hotel.

Broad Street in 1984, before the redevelopment started, had become very shabby as can be seen from this photograph. Looking towards Five Ways, Quayside Tower can be seen in the distance which has since been refurbished, and the corner of Bridge Street with the Rendezvous Café is now the site of the landmark Hyatt hotel, linked across Broad Street by a bridge, to the International Convention Centre. One of the original ornamental street lamps can also be seen on the corner of King Alfred's Place. The pedestrian crossing still remains albeit on the other side of Bridge Street.

In the late 1960s the former ATV television studios moved from Lichfield Road in Aston (later home to the BRMB Radio studios) to this city centre site bordering Bridge Street and Holliday Street. Later it became known as the Central Television Studios where well known programmes such as 'Crossroads' and 'The Golden Shot' were produced. The car-park in the distance has remained closed for many years after one of similar construction in Wolverhampton collapsed due to structural defects. The studios moved to smaller premises in nearby Gas Street in the 1990s and the whole area is scheduled for redevelopment in the near future.

Bingley Hall in King Alfred's Place in 1977. It was built in 1849 on the site of the former Bingley House which was demolished way back in 1830; never-ending renewal is nothing new in the city. It was the first purpose-built exhibition hall in Great Britain, constructed using surplus steel girders from the building of Euston station in London. During its life it was home to Dog Shows, Cattle Shows, Circuses, Pop Concerts and so on. It would turn its hand to anything and in January 1984, while the Midland Caravan and Camping Exhibition was taking place, a serious fire broke out and destroyed most of the interior of the building. Demolition followed shortly afterwards with the site quickly redeveloped to become the home of the Birmingham International Convention Centre, which was opened by Her Majesty the Queen on 12th June 1991. To date the centre has hosted events such as political conferences, concerts and in 1998 the Eurovision Song Contest which might have had some people looking fondly back on the days of the Midland Caravan and Camping Exhibition!

Looking north up the West Coast main line out of New Street station, with the St. Vincent Street bridge in the background in 1988. The view shows the area now occupied by the National Indoor Arena (NIA). By this time the scrap yard to the right had already been vacated in preparation for construction of the NIA. The listed entrance, at the end of the original New Street station tunnel, is now hidden as the NIA building which covers this site has now extended the tunnel up to the St. Vincent Street bridge. When first constructed there was talk of building a railway station beneath the NIA, but its close proximity to the main New Street station eventually saw it ruled it out. The NIA has an insulated floor to absorb the vibration from passing trains. The Arena was a welcome addition to the International Convention Centre complex and has over the years been the venue for numerous pop concerts and sporting events. Recently, plans have been announced to update the NIA to bring the centre up to modern day standards, which will substantially alter its appearance.

The Royal Mail sorting office in Navigation Street, completed in 1970, remained the home of the Royal Mail in Birmingham until 1998, when its operations moved to a new state-of-the-art building in Newtown. The former premises have since been converted (involving demolition of all but the steel sub-structure) into a mixed use development of two hotels, offices, apartments and a shopping arcade with restaurants and bars, and the whole complex is now known as – 'The Mailbox'. Once again a former existence lives on (somewhat pointlessly) only in a name. In 2004 the BBC in Birmingham moved into the centre from their former home at Pebble Mill (shown elsewhere in this book)

and today all local and current affairs programmes are broadcast from these studios. A new structure to complement The Mailbox, known as 'The Cube' has now been built at the canal basin end of the building, clad in bronze coloured steel and glass and home to more apartments and restaurants. There was no obvious origin around which to weave a name – at least 'The Cube' recognises what the thing is! This photograph taken in 1998 shows the front of the Royal Mail building in its original form before the above mentioned transformation began. A large staircase leading into 'The Mailbox' now occupies this area.

Davenports was a well known Birmingham name dating back to 1815. Bottling of stout began at the Bath Street site in 1920 and the building was greatly extended in the 1930s as demand for the ales increased. Famous for its 'Beer at Home' slogan, the company had a fleet of vans to deliver drinks to your doorstep and collect the empty bottles! This would attract a measure opprobrium you'd suspect, amid today's binge-drink concerns but it was fairly commonplace across the country – and of course milk and soft drinks were home-delivered too. During 1989 the company was taken over by Greenall Whitley who closed the brewery and moved production to Burton-Upon-Trent with the loss of 100 jobs. This 1993 view shows the former offices/bottling store/garages shortly before the bulldozers moved in. Birmingham City Council applied to give the building listed status, but the Department of the Environment rejected the request. Birmingham College of Food, Tourism and Creative Studies, who bought the site, have now built a six storey student accommodation block on the land with 354 bedrooms, along with other apartment blocks.

The entrance to Smallbrook Queensway in 1982, looking towards the Bull Ring and showing the corner building housing the AEEW union offices with Gino's restaurant below. The site was cleared some years ago to make way for the 38 storey Radison SAS hotel which now occupies this site. Above the hotel are numerous luxury apartments with a penthouse suite at the top. This landmark building, finished in a random light green glazed effect, overlooks the Holloway Circus roundabout from where this picture was taken. The shrubs in the centre have now been replaced by a 'pagoda' style tower, promoting the nearby Chinese Quarter. When the pagoda, paid for by a local entrepreneur, was first installed there were concerns about its weight on the underpass which runs beneath. Extra supports have now been added in the underpass which can be seen when driving through on the A38.

Originally this area was scheduled for office development and the plan got as far as an artist's impression being erected on the site. However the scheme never materialised and this view of the corner of Navigation Street and John Bright Street shows the buildings in 2000 before they were swept away for apartments (when did we stop calling them 'flats'?) known as the Orion building. The facade of the four storey building in John Bright Street has been kept and incorporated into the new complex. The Mailbox Shopping Centre can be seen in the background under green netting as work continued to convert the building from a mail sorting centre into the current upmarket shopping centre.

Opposite the Town Hall are the remains of the old Central Library shortly before this final section was demolished in 1984. Its replacement can be seen in the background. This site is now occupied by a garden area rather than a building; indeed many buildings planned for the Paradise Circus development were never built. A bus station beneath the complex *was* built but never used. Today a new library has been put up on the car park area between Baskerville House and the Repertory Theatre in Broad Street, with the current library set to be demolished and redeveloped as part of a £600m gateway project to the Broad Street area. Prince Charles described the new building, put up during 1969-1972, as a 'giant carbuncle' but his National Gallery-style intervention did not work this time. Despite many peoples' efforts, in November 2009 it was denied grade 2 listed status and the above-mentioned scheme is now due to go ahead.

The Central Library in 1974 shortly after completion, before other nearby buildings were added to it as part of a greater Paradise Circus project. As mentioned earlier the full complex never materialised and land earmarked for the project was sold off, for the Copthorne Hotel and Chamberlain House. The original library had opened in 1865 on a site nearby but it was more or less destroyed in 1879 when a fire broke out during the construction of an extension, with the loss of 50,000 books. The rebuilt library opened in 1882 but by 1938 ever more books meant a replacement was necessary. The Second World War intervened and it was not until 1960, when a new Inner Ring Road was in prospect, that plans for the new library were drawn up; construction began in 1969.

The day the 'City of Birmingham' moved! Well, not really. To mark the beginning of the new millennium many cities undertook major building projects, London's Dome for instance, and Portsmouth's Spinnaker Tower. Birmingham's project was slightly more practical than either in that a building called Millennium Point was constructed on Curzon Street as a replacement for the Science Museum in Newhall Street. This had long outgrown its original premises and over the years had found itself using several buildings. On 2nd December 2000 46235, the former LMS Coronation class Pacific locomotive, is being moved out of its home of over 30 years en-route to its new home at Millennium Point. The tender followed on a separate trailer. 'City of Birmingham' is now positioned so that the public can walk through the cab of the locomotive, although many railway enthusiasts would love to see her back in steam on the main line – maybe one day! The museum is also home to Birmingham's last tram and many other engineering and scientific artefacts associated with Birmingham's history, with many interactive displays, and is well worth a visit.

In 1977, the Queen's Silver Jubilee year, many buildings around the city were decorated to commemorate the occasion. This scene in Victoria Square showing the open grassed area, before the fountains were built, shows the decorated Town Hall and the crowds gathering to see the Queen as she left after her visit to the city. Recently the Town Hall has undergone a major refurbishment using lottery funding to bring this Grade 1 listed building back to its former glory both inside and out. The process took three years, the Town Hall fully re-opening in 2008.

The National Exhibition Centre just outside Birmingham at Bickenhill, opened in January 1976. Two years later the prestigious bi-annual Motor Show, which had always been held at Earls Court in London, moved to the NEC, occupying the original five halls, with many external displays. The show continued every two years from 1978 to 2002, when due to falling attendance figures (930,000 in 1978 to 650,000 in 2002) the Society of Motor Manufacturers and Traders decided to move the show back to London, this time to the new East London Exhibition Centre in the Docklands area. This view taken in 1980 shows the exhibits and street-lamp banners placed around the city centre to promote the event, with the (then) Birmingham-built Minis taking pride of place. In the background can be seen the Lloyds Bank building, since demolished and replaced by a more stylish office block. The former Nat-West Bank tower behind is also scheduled for redevelopment. Ironically the SMMT has now decided to abandon the Motor Show altogether.

Looking down New Street towards Corporation Street in 2001, on the corner of Temple Street we see the former Temple House, shortly before its demolition. The building was a 1960s modernised version of the original. Today the corner site is home to a Tesco store with an apartment block above. There are now a number of small supermarkets in the city centre, serving the needs of the ever increasing numbers who now live there in the new apartment blocks.

New Street has always been the city's main thoroughfare and shopping area. In 1991, like many other towns and cities, the street and some others were pedestrianised, with traffic excluded. This is New Street shortly before the cars, buses and lorries were banished; today the road is a tree-lined, block-paved area with street entertainers – a futuristic information office built in 2004 now occupies the site in the foreground.

Corporation Street in December 1984, when the traffic ran the opposite way to what it did in recent times. The Christmas decorations that year were relatively simple, but more colourful than the ones we have today. The C&A store can be seen on the right. In 2012 all traffic was removed from Corporation Street in preparation for the Metro Tramway extension from Snow Hill station to New Street station.

Corporation Street, looking towards New Street in 1991, showing the former New Victoria Hotel building on the corner of Union Street, with the C&A store in the background. The hotel occupied the floors above the shops with an entrance on the corner opposite C&A. The building was pulled down in 1994 and a new period style apartment complex was completed in 1996. As before, there are shops on the ground floor level. The buildings in the foreground have also been refurbished as part of the Martineau Square upgrade project.

The corner of Temple Street and Cherry Street, seen from the St. Philips churchyard, in 1974. The former Midland Bank had just been demolished, enabling this view of the shops in Cherry Street. These succumbed in turn to the bulldozer some years later, and the site is now home to a Lloyds Bank with offices above. The large Rackhams (now House of Fraser) department store can be seen in the background.

With the Grand Hotel in the background, this picture shows the buildings on the corner of Livery Street and Colmore Row in 1986. The site was cleared in 1987 and is now home to a Barclays Bank. The Grand Hotel has now closed; structural problems made its future uncertain but in 2004 this French Renaissance building, dating from 1875, has now been granted listed status. Its future, if not as a hotel, is thus assured, and work is well underway on its refurbishment.

Snow Hill station opened in 1852 and was rebuilt in 1912 into the station of such fond memory to so many of us. Built by the Great Western Railway as Birmingham's station on the Paddington to Birkenhead line, apart from damage during the Second World War, the place remained much the same until closure in 1972, although the Hotel fronting Colmore Row had been demolished some years earlier. The former trackbed areas were subsequently used for car parking until 1977 when the entire site was knocked down. The current multi-storey car park and station were constructed in the 1980s and the new station opened in 1987 with train services extended from Moor Street, and later through to Stourbridge. The opening was marked on 12th September 1987 by allowing the public to walk through the half mile long tunnel from Moor Street, an event in which I took part. On 31st May 1999 the Midland Metro tramway system opened and took over a platform on the Snow Hill side of the station. It runs from Wolverhampton on the former Great Western trackbed, though the tramway is now scheduled to be extended round the city centre, vacating this platform once again. This view taken in 1975, looking down Livery Street from the junction at Barwick Street, shows the side elevation of the station. A part of the original tile-glazed brick wall with two GWR emblems on it has been retained; this is further down the hill in this picture. The current entrance to the multi-storey car park is marked by the large arches. The offices on the left have also been replaced, by a modern office block.

This was the view from the top of the multi-storey car park above Snow Hill station in 2003, showing the St. Chads road island on the inner ring-road, before it was redeveloped in 2007/8. The Kennedy memorial mosaic is at the bottom of the picture, and part of the Snow Hill station mosaic can be seen on the walls of the sunken gardens. St. Chads cathedral in the background remains the same, but the road layout is now in the form of a staggered 'T' junction with ground level pedestrian crossings and traffic light controlled junctions. The present dual carriageway runs either side of the tunnel ventilator box below the fir trees.

The pedestrian subways of the 1960s were another town planning notion which foundered on the rocks of grim reality. Pedestrians were forced underground to allow traffic to flow freely above, in a pernicious reversal of priorities. In recent years wiser counsels have prevailed and the city has set about removing many of these warrens. Over the years they have become a mugger's paradise and many were regularly defaced with graffiti. The sunken garden area at St. Chads remained fairly unscathed and was home to two mosaics, one set in a fountain pool, in memory of J. F. Kennedy, and one as a memorial to the sadly missed Snow Hill Station depicting its history until 1972 when the station closed. The Kennedy mosaic has been saved and in its slightly modified form relocated in the corner of Floodgate Street in the Digbeth area, but sadly the entire station mosaic has been destroyed with the new road layout of St. Chads Circus. The location of the Great Western Castle Class locomotive is now the foundation area of a forty storey apartment complex – itself presently halted by deterioration in the property market.

The junction of Bull Street and Colmore Row, and the former Greys department store building, which in later years was taken over by Debenhams. Hamleys then ran it for a number of years as a large toy store, only to finally vacate the premises in the late 1980s. The building was finally demolished in 1990 and the site is now occupied by Colmore Gate, a multi-storey office complex finished in black marble. The vacant site adjacent to the building used to be a branch of Boots the chemist, demolished in the 1960s. The land remained empty for some years and, under the ownership of Debenhams, a loading bay area was built on the site. The subway beneath the road in the foreground has since been removed with the redevelopment of Colmore Circus.

Colmore Circus, Matthew Boulton's birthplace (1728) is one of the most redeveloped areas of the city centre with all the buildings surrounding the square having been replaced or modernised. The Wesleyan & General offices (seen here in 1980) followed the line of the original Steelhouse Lane which was cut short when Colmore Circus was constructed in the 1960s. A new iconic Wesleyan & General building now occupies this site, and Colmore Plaza, a 12 storey office block stands where the Post and Mail offices used to be.

The Post and Mail building in Colmore Circus in 2003. It was completed in 1964 and remained the home of the 'Birmingham Post' and 'Evening Mail' newspapers until 2004 when they moved out to a new site at Fort Dunlop. The 220ft office tower received praise at the time for its stylish design but two attempts to give it listed status were unsuccessful. Demolition began during 2005 using hydraulic excavators, rather than controlled explosions, due to the close proximity of other buildings. Construction of the current 'Colmore Plaza' office complex began in 2006 and was completed in 2008. The remaining office and print room area of the Post and Mail complex in Weaman Street was demolished in 2013.

Still in Colmore Circus, in 1996, with Dr Johnson House, at the rear of the former Lewis store, built in the 1960s. The smaller office block at the end, home to the 'Brown Derby' public house in the basement, was added later. The building succumbed to the wrecking ball (well, a hydraulic grab at any rate) some years later, and a new multi-storey office block now squats here. The road to the right is now part of a pedestrianised square and the subway in the foreground has been removed and replaced by a ground level pelican crossing. In the background is the office block which replaced the former Greys/Debenhams building.

The Old Square was rebuilt in the 1960s as part of the 'Inner Ring Road Scheme' otherwise known as Priory Ringway, linking Colmore and Masshouse Circus 'islands'. Once again the traffic was kept above ground and pedestrians condemned, Morlock-like, to the subways below. As a result the Old Square was turned into the 'sunken garden' (don't laugh) pictured here. Behind was a bronze mural commemorating the history of the Old Square, sculpted by Kenneth Budd in 1967, and the rest of the area was filled with shops and er, public toilets. Some years after this picture was taken in 1996, the area was filled in and brought up to ground level again. A statue in memory of Hall Green born comedian Tony Hancock now resides in the square, opposite the relocated aforesaid mural with eight street lamps which used to stand in other parts of the city.

The view east from the Dale House car park in 2000, along the A47 towards Saltley, showing the 1960s Masshouse Circus, one of the many 'road islands' on the Inner Ring Road. This one was unusual as it was built entirely on concrete pillars. The area below was used for a rather dreary ground level car park. In 2002 the island was demolished, and the area has now been completely redeveloped with a ground level road system, and two multi-storey apartment blocks now occupy the ground level car park in the distance. A new Matthew Boulton College (now known as The Birmingham Metropolitan College), occupies the land adjacent to the Aston University buildings. Dale House and car park are also scheduled for demolition, to make way for a new shopping development to breathe new life into this north-east corner of the city centre.

With Millennium Point in the background, this view from Albert Street shows the buildings on the corner of Chapel Street, in 2000. With the removal of the elevated Masshouse Circus, Chapel Street, once a quiet side road was, for a short time, part of the main road network in the area. The road has since disappeared and is now part of the new Eastside City Park which opened in 2012 and stretches in front of Millennium Point. The former TNT depot opposite and these buildings have been demolished to make way for the park which was cut down in size to allow for the proposed High Speed railway station.

Cardigan Street in 2004, looking towards Belmont Row, won't mean much to the general public at present but this area is set to become part of the 'Eastside' project. This has created a new city centre park in front of Millennium Point. Now all these buildings have been demolished except the Victorian works, in the distance. A listed structure dating from 1899, it was badly damaged by fire some years later. Work on this site began in 2010 with a new Birmingham City University complex now occupying this area. More recently a new high speed rail terminal has been incorporated into the plans making use of land close to the old Curzon Street railway building, the original terminus of the railway from London Euston.

High Street from the base of the Rotunda in 1986, with the former Co-op which used to occupy both sides of the road, linked by an underground passage. The store closed in 1986 and was demolished to make way for the Pavilions Shopping Centre. The buildings on the opposite side of the road still remain, albeit as separate shops and have recently been modernised, and the Times furnishing store is now a Waterstones bookshop linked into the shopping centre. Traffic is no longer allowed into this area and the foreground now forms the approach to the new BullRing Shopping Centre, with the famous bronze bull statue.

The city end of Digbeth in 1988, with Park Street on the right and the ten storey St. Martins House, a typical 1960s office block with adjoining multi storey car-park. The entrance into the old Bull Ring underground car-park can be seen at the centre of the picture marked by the 'P' sign. Park Street now forms the main thoroughfare around the new BullRing complex and this area is now home to the Selfridges department store, with the former Digbeth dual carriageway now part of the pedestrianised walkway leading into the shopping centre.

The Bull Ring in 1988 and the popular outdoor market, with the main buildings behind. When first opened, Woolworths occupied the main shop frontage to the left of the picture, and the Bull Ring Centre logo used to be positioned at the JVC end of the building. The Fuji-Film illuminated advertisement at the top of the multi-storey office block could be seen fifteen miles away from the M6 motorway on the approach to Birmingham from London. Today, only the Rotunda survives (converted into apartments from an office block in 2006) and that we see here is now within the new BullRing Centre.

The Bull Ring used to have a small area garden area known as the Manzoni Gardens, seen here on a sunny day in 1997; for a number of years it was home to a statue of King Kong! The sunken gardens were built on the site of the former Bull Ring fish market which lost its roof during the Second World War and was finally demolished in 1963. The area now forms the western end of the current BullRing centre, home to Debenhams. The bridge linking the Bull Ring to the Pallasades Shopping Centre is just visible in the background, and is one of the few remaining parts of the original Bull Ring, although heavily modified.

Birmingham's original Bull Ring was the first undercover shopping centre to be built in Britain, and was opened by the Duke of Edinburgh, Prince Philip on 29th May 1964. It was host to 140 shop units inside and 150 stalls in the outside market in front of the centre. This view just off the main Centre-Court shows how dated the place looked by 2000. The rooflight windows were added some years after the Bull Ring's construction, to let natural light in to the complex. The centre was demolished soon after and this area is now part of the Debenhams department store.

Inside the Bull Ring Centre in 1997 with the stairs leading from the bridge across Smallbrook Queensway, into the main Shopping Centre. The small café pictured here overlooked the main Centre Court below. The bridge linking the Pallasades Shopping Centre to the Bull Ring still remains, but the area in this photograph is now given over to one of the entrances into the Debenhams department store.

A busy scene on a Saturday in 1985 and the Bull Ring outdoor market is in its final form, with covered steel roofs. At first the arrangements were more traditional with small canvas covered stalls. Taken from the ramp which used to link the upper level of the Bull Ring, the view shows the rear of the Co-op store on High Street , with the Times Furnishing building alongside. The corner of the main Bull Ring building can be seen in the foreground. The Pavilions Shopping Centre now sits on the Co-op site, and the very popular Bull Ring outdoor market has been re-sited on the other side of Edgbaston Street. The foreground now forms the open area in front of St. Martins church, alongside the iconic Selfridges building.

The old Bull Ring again, this time looking up Edgbaston Street towards Pershore Street, in 1990. The road formed the southern end of the complex with many bus stops along its length. The multi-storey car park at the top of the centre was to have an American-style car parking system where cars moved between floors on lifts. However the idea proved unsuccessful and the car park remained an unused white elephant until demolition in 2000. Today the street remains, albeit pedestrianised, forming the main thoroughfare between the back of the new BullRing centre and the new indoor markets to the left of the picture.

Edgbaston Street, at the rear of the Bull Ring, in 1974 showing the office end of the former Birmingham Wholesale Market in Jamaica Row, with the St. Martins public house on the corner. Demolition had already begun, and today the only buildings remaining are those in the distance at the rear of Digbeth, and the back of St. Martin's cathedral. The new open-air BullRing market now occupies this area, and Jamaica Row has completely disappeared.

This view of Jamaica Row, towards the Bull Ring in 1973, taken from the junction with Bromsgrove Street and Moat Row, illustrates the size of the old Birmingham Wholesale Market. St. Martins Cathedral spire can be seen just above the market buildings. This area is now within the walls of the current wholesale market site, which opened in 1976, although talks are currently taking place about a new wholesale market being built in the Witton area of Birmingham on the former IMI site. This plan has upset the BullRing market traders who will have to get their produce from Witton if the plan goes ahead, rather than fetching it from across the road as happens at present. Note the 1960s cars in the shape of a Mini, Ford Anglia and a Morris Minor in the distance.

In the early 1960s a one-way, steel, single-track flyover was erected at the southern end of Digbeth to ease traffic flow at the junction of the A34 Stratford Road and A45 Coventry Road. Meant only as a temporary construction the flyover lasted 28 years with double-decker buses just being able to squeeze over it. The structure, seen here in 1989 from the city end, was taken down shortly afterwards, replaced by a more conventional traffic-light controlled junction.

Matthew Boulton College, opened in the late 1960s, was situated at the junction of Bristol Street and Belgrave Middleway. The college is named after the famous manufacturer and business partner of James Watt. He was among the prominent Birmingham men of the Lunar Society, enamoured of the newly-emerging arts, sciences, and theology. The Society met each month near the full moon! The college has recently moved to a 'state of the art' complex near Aston University. The office block-style building seen here in 2005 has now been demolished, unusually by a hydraulic grab rather than explosives; cost was given as the reason.

In the 1960s Birmingham's answer to replacing numerous run-down terraced houses was to build high-rise tower blocks, many of them to a design like the one pictured here. The twenty storey Haddon Tower was built in 1967 with 119 flats, on the junction of Bristol Street and Lee Bank Middleway. It was the last remaining block of many on the Lee Bank estate. By this time many such blocks had fallen very much out of favour and on Sunday 23 July 2006, Haddon Tower was demolished using controlled explosives after only fourteen weeks of preparation. The entire area up to Broad Street has since been rebuilt and is known as the 'Park Central' scheme with smaller housing units and apartment blocks. This corner area is being considered as a future supermarket development. One of the unpopular subways can be seen in the foreground.

The Birmingham Mint was formed from Matthew Boulton and James Watt's Soho Mint. With Matthew Boulton's innovative ideas the Mint became one of the foremost factories of its day using steam to power the equipment. The works were frequently modernised during its 209 year history, and there were even plans to extend the factory on the opposite side of Icknield Street as recently as the 1990s. Sadly, however, in 2003 the Birmingham Mint went into liquidation and the site was sold for redevelopment. The picture shows the buildings in 2005 shortly before partial demolition. The office buildings in the distance have been retained whilst the rest of the site has been redeveloped into apartments built around the chimney stack – which also remains as a landmark of the development.

The former Great Western Railway goods depot at Hockley was one of the country's largest in its heyday. With the closure of Snow Hill station in 1972 the site became redundant and much of the area was made into an industrial estate. This view in 1991 shows the low bridge (almost a tunnel) over Icknield Street which carried the tracks of the goods yard. It was only just high enough for double-decker buses to pass beneath. The former Great Western Offices are on the left. The widening of the Ring Road to a dual carriageway saw their demolition, along with the low bridge. The base section of the offices still remains whilst a new bridge now spans the road, but it is of course not nearly so lengthy, carrying just two railway lines, from Snow Hill to Stourbridge, and two tram lines from Snow Hill to Wolverhampton known as the Midland Metro. The walls have also been rebuilt, in a railway architectural style.

Lucas was a well known Birmingham based company producing electrical components for the motor trade, with factories in Acocks Green, Hockley and the one pictured here in Lozells. The nearby works in Great Hampton Street, Hockley has been converted into luxury apartments now known as the New Hampton Lofts. The Lozells site, seen here in 1985, was demolished in the 1990s and is now home to much smaller industrial units. Lucas still continues in Birmingham under the name of TRW Electronics.

In the mid-1980s Birmingham organised Formula 3 Motor Racing around the city streets based on the Bristol Street/Belgrave Road area. Special crash-barriers were erected around the course with the pits at (appropriately!) Monaco House in Bristol Street. The first race took place in torrential rain and after a few more years it was decided that the cost and inconvenience was unacceptable and the event was abandoned. Today there are still reminders of its existence, in the peculiar shape of the road island on Highgate Middleway for instance. Moreover every spring, bulbs planted on the Bristol Street site opposite Monaco House grow up through the grass to read 'Birmingham Super Prix' This is a race in October 1984 looking down Belgrave Middleway with the now demolished Matthew Boulton College and Haddon Tower in the background. In more recent years talks have taken place about re-instating the event to help promote Birmingham but to date, there has been no further progress.

Ken's Café in 1987, on the corner of Station Road and Witton Lane. It leads a line of semi-detached houses that were demolished in the early 1990s so that the adjacent Aston Villa Football ground could be extended with the construction of the 'Doug Ellis Stand'. The current Witton Lane occupies the site of these former houses whilst the new stand was built over the old road area. Previously known as the Witton Road stand, many Villa fans objected to it being renamed after the club's longstanding Chairman 'Deadly Doug' Doug Ellis, although he claimed to knew nothing about it, until after it had happened. The Aston Villa ground was host to three games during the famous 1966 World Cup. With further improvements, the ground held some football matches during the 2012 Olympic Games.

Built in 1961 the three tower blocks at Perry Barr (Tweed, Birchfield and Calder) were landmarks on the A34 Walsall Road, replacing innumerable old terraced houses in the area. These tower blocks were seen as the answer to the housing needs at the time, but over the years they became unloved and expensive to maintain due to vandalism and anti-social behaviour. Identical blocks in Newtown were refurbished in 2000 and originally these three blocks were due to be upgraded by 'Urban Splash' and converted into apartments. However the recession rendered the scheme financially impractical and as a result two of the blocks were demolished between January and June 2010 using a hydraulic grab, owing to the close proximity to the A34 Walsall Road. Birchfield Tower survived until 2011 because of a mobile telephone mast on the roof but it was pulled down once the mast was relocated. The site is set to become a small housing estate with affordable homes for local residents.

HP Sauce has been produced in Birmingham since 1896 and was so named when its inventor Frederick Gibson Garton, a grocer from Nottingham, heard that it was being served in the Houses of Parliament. The factory was cut in two by the A38(M) Expressway in the 1960s requiring a pipeline to be constructed over the road from the Tower Road factory site which produced the vinegar. In 2005 Heinz purchased the parent company HP Foods from Danone, and despite a referral to the Office of Fair Trading, the £440 million takeover deal was agreed in April 2006. In May 2006 Heinz announced plans to move production of HP Sauce from its Aston site to its European Sauces factory in Elst in the Netherlands. A fight to save the factory ensued including a boycott of Heinz products but by 16 March 2007 the battle was lost and the factory closed with the loss of 125 jobs. Local MPs and many others have tried to insist that the sauce bottles should no longer carry the Houses of Parliament image as the product was no longer made in Great Britain but to date it still appears on the bottles. Pictured on a sunny November morning in 2006, the demolition of the site began in July 2007, with the entire site cleared soon afterwards. One of the large HP Sauce signs which used to overlook the A38(M) has been saved and put on display at the recently re-opened MAC Arts Centre. It may be relocated on the site when rebuilt, as a memorial to the works. Part of the site is now home to food warehouses. The ornate clock tower previously stood outside the Ansells Brewery but was relocated (see next) here on the road island at the junction of Rocky Lane/Park Lane and Lichfield Road.

Joseph Ansell founded the Aston Cross Brewery in 1858 and Ansells became a limited company in 1901. It grew over the next 40 years with the acquisition of many smaller breweries including the Holt Brewery in 1934. Holt's logo, a red squirrel in side profile, was subsequently adopted by Ansells to identify its own beers. In 1961 Ansells merged with Taylor Walker and Ind Coope to form Allied Breweries. Following an industrial dispute the brewery closed in 1981with production moving to Allied's Burton-Upon-Trent plant, bringing to an end 100 years of brewing in Birmingham. Some former staff set up the Aston Manor Brewery in nearby Nechells. When this photograph was taken in 1987 the large Ansells sign had already been removed. To the left can be seen the HP Sauce factory. Both buildings have since disappeared, the Ansells site now occupied by various car showrooms, and the HP Sauce site is scheduled to be home to a warehouse and a hotel. The clock tower is in its original position before being moved to the new site on the Lichfield Road/Rocky Lane road island – see previous view.

Misguidedly, the city built many – too many – tower blocks and many in turn became unpopular, some for structural problems. These three blocks at Chelmsley Wood were 'system built' using pre-manufactured panels put together like a kit, and were more prone to damp than earlier brick built structures. As a result many have now been demolished, and this picture taken at 12.00 noon on 26 February 1989 shows the final moments of three tower blocks after a controlled demolition by explosives. The site is now occupied by a housing estate.

BBC Pebble Mill Studios in Edgbaston in June 2004. They were built in 1967 and opened by Princess Anne on 10 November 1971. The seven storey building contained offices, a television studio, a radio studio, canteens and gardens. The world's longest running radio soap 'The Archers' was produced at Pebble Mill, as were talk shows 'Pebble Mill at One', 'Good Morning with Anne and Nick' , 'Midlands Today' and numerous TV dramas. After changes in the way TV was produced, combined with increased maintenance costs of the 1960s building, a decision was taken to move to the 'Mailbox' in the city centre, a process completed by October 2004. Remaining fixtures and fittings were auctioned off at Pebble Mill during November and the studios were demolished between May and September 2005. The site is set to become a 'science park' linked to the nearby Birmingham University, but so far only an entrance onto the A38 Bristol Road has been built. More recently the area is being considered for the relocation of the Dental Hospital, from it current site in the city centre.

The Longbridge car plant opened in 1905, founded by Herbert Austin. Car production was interrupted during the two World Wars when the factory switched to guns, ammunition, tanks and so on. After the Second World War Austin amalgamated with the Morris and became the BMC, British Motor Corporation, which in 1968 became known as British Leyland. During 1975 the company ran into financial difficulties and received help from the government, who renamed the company BL. During the 1970s a total of 523 industrial disputes nearly destroyed the company but in 1979 a new assembly line to build the Austin Metro was constructed, with the car launched in 1980. The car proved a huge success and was re-branded under the Rover marque in 1990 after the company was sold to British Aerospace. For the next five years a new series of Rover cars was launched (Rover 200/400 etc.). In 1994 BMW took over Rover to help its worldwide sales, but shareholders prevailed and in 2000 Rover was sold to the Phoenix Consortium for £10! By April 2005 despite efforts to keep the company afloat, the MG Rover Group went into administration with the loss of 6000 jobs. The Nanjing Chinese Automobile Association bought Rover three months later and in August 2008, production of a new sports car, the MGTF began, using a small part of the old Austin southern works on the Rednal Road, employing around 200 people. This photograph taken in 2006 looking towards Rednal shows the Rover and MG badges, the final brands of cars produced at the plant. All these buildings have now been demolished apart from the Cofton Park end of the site mentioned earlier. In 2013 the remains of a 1976 Mini Clubman were found in one of the numerous tunnels linking various parts of the works, built during the Second World War as bomb shelters. The Mini thus earned the title 'Last Car to Leave the Factory' and although in poor condition was duly auctioned off!

Longbridge again, this time looking towards the city centre along the A38 Bristol Road showing the original West Works complex, the oldest part of the site. All these buildings were demolished shortly after the photograph was taken in 2006, and at present the whole area is subject to a multi-million re-generation scheme consisting of retail, office, manufacturing and housing development, and a museum of car manufacture in Birmingham. The scheme got the go-ahead in February 2009, and a feasibility study to re-open the former Halesowen branch railway line as far as Frankley in Birmingham is being considered.